The Pledge of Allegiance

by Kirsten Chang

BELLWETHER MEDIA • MINNEAPOLIS, MN

Note to Librarians, Teachers, and Parents:

Blastoff! Readers are carefully developed by literacy experts and combine standards-based content with developmentally appropriate text.

Level 1 provides the most support through repetition of high-frequency words, light text, predictable sentence patterns, and strong visual support.

Level 2 offers early readers a bit more challenge through varied simple sentences, increased text load, and less repetition of high-frequency words.

Level 3 advances early-fluent readers toward fluency through increased text and concept load, less reliance on visuals, longer sentences, and more literary language.

Level 4 builds reading stamina by providing more text per page, increased use of punctuation, greater variation in sentence patterns, and increasingly challenging vocabulary.

Level 5 encourages children to move from "learning to read" to "reading to learn" by providing even more text, varied writing styles, and less familiar topics.

Whichever book is right for your reader, Blastoff! Readers are the perfect books to build confidence and encourage a love of reading that will last a lifetime!

This edition first published in 2019 by Bellwether Media, Inc.

No part of this publication may be reproduced in whole or in part without written permission of the publisher. For information regarding permission, write to Bellwether Media, Inc., Attention: Permissions Department, 6012 Blue Circle Drive, Minnetonka, MN 55343.

Library of Congress Cataloging-in-Publication Data

Names: Chang, Kristen, author.
Title: The Pledge of Allegiance / by Kristen Chang.
Description: Minneapolis, MN : Bellwether Media, Inc., 2019. | Series: Blastoff! Readers. Symbols of American Freedom | Includes bibliographical references and index.
Identifiers: LCCN 2017061636 (print) | LCCN 2018005272 (ebook) | ISBN 9781626178854 (hardcover : alk. paper) | ISBN 9781618914712 (pbk. : alk. paper) | ISBN 9781681035482 (ebook)
Subjects: LCSH: Bellamy, Francis. Pledge of Allegiance to the Flag–History–Juvenile literature. | Flags–United States–History–Juvenile literature.
Classification: LCC JC346 (ebook) | LCC JC346 .C43 2019 (print) | DDC 323.6/5–dc23 LC record available at https://lccn.loc.gov/2017061636

Editor: Rebecca Sabelko   Designer: Andrea Schneider

Printed in the United States of America, North Mankato, MN.

Table of Contents

What Is the Pledge of Allegiance?

Americans say the **Pledge** of **Allegiance** to honor their country.

4

They stand
and place their
right hands over
their hearts.

Saying the Pledge shows belief in **freedom**. It shows belief in fairness.

A Long History

Francis Bellamy wrote the Pledge in 1892. It first appeared in a kids' magazine.

What the Pledge Promises

- Honor the flag

- Believe in our country

- Everyone sticks together

- Everyone is free and equal

Later, **Congress** made it a **symbol** for freedom.

Since then, it has changed a little. New words were added.

Who Says It?

Americans say the Pledge to respect the flag.

Lawmakers say it at meetings. People say it in schools.

The Pledge tells us we live in the land of the free!

Glossary

allegiance
loyalty

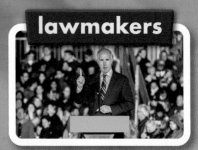
lawmakers
people who make rules for a country

Congress
the group of people who make the rules for the United States

pledge
a promise or agreement

freedom
the state of being free

symbol
something that stands for something else

To Learn More

AT THE LIBRARY

Carr, Aaron. *Pledge of Allegiance*. New York, N.Y.: Smartbook Media Inc., 2017.

Chang, Kirsten. *The United States Flag*. Minneapolis, Minn.: Bellwether Media, 2019.

Raum, Elizabeth. *The Pledge of Allegiance in Translation: What It Really Means*. North Mankato, Minn.: Capstone Press, 2018.

ON THE WEB

Learning more about the Pledge of Allegiance is as easy as 1, 2, 3.

1. Go to www.factsurfer.com.

2. Enter "Pledge of Allegiance" into the search box.

3. Click the "Surf" button and you will see a list of related web sites.

With factsurfer.com, finding more information is just a click away.

Index